THE ENCHANTED ROOM

THE

ENCHANTED

ROOM

POEMS BY

MAURYA SIMON

COPPER CANYON PRESS

THE PUBLICATION OF THIS BOOK IS MADE POSSIBLE BY A
GRANT FROM THE NATIONAL ENDOWMENT FOR THE ARTS.

COPPER CANYON PRESS IS IN RESIDENCE WITH CENTRUM
AT FORT WORDEN STATE PARK.

ISBN: 0-914742-98-1
LIBRARY OF CONGRESS CATALOG CARD NUMBER: 86-71839
COPYRIGHT © 1986 BY MAURYA SIMON
ALL RIGHTS RESERVED.

THE TYPE IS GALLIARD, DESIGNED BY MATTHEW CARTER
BOOK DESIGNED BY TREE SWENSON

FRONTISPIECE BY BAILA GOLDENTHAL
"INVERSIONS" (PHOTOGRAPHED BY JOHN THOMPSON)
1980; MIXED MEDIA, 66 × 42″
(DETAIL OF THE PAINTING ON COVER)

COPPER CANYON PRESS
POST OFFICE BOX 271
PORT TOWNSEND, WASHINGTON 98368

Grateful acknowledgment is given the following periodicals in which these poems originally appeared:

ANEMONE: Garden Twilight
CALIFORNIA QUARTERLY: Venice, 1959
THE CUMBERLAND POETRY REVIEW: Snapshot
CUTBANK: Madras Insomnia
DARING POETRY QUARTERLY: The Enchanted Room
ELECTRUM: Seizure
ELEPHANT-EAR: The Soldier, Wintering In
GRAND STREET: The Sibyl
GROVE MAGAZINE: The Origin of Death
KANSAS QUARTERLY: Winter Song
THE LITERARY REVIEW: Hermosa Beach, Revisited
THE LITTLE MAGAZINE: On the Island of Krk, Red Tide
MANHATTAN POETRY REVIEW: November Ellipsis
MOSAIC: Blue Movies, Still Life in Kitchen, Heat Wave,
    Dividing the Light, The Burning Rose, Night, Volga Tale
NATIONAL FEDERATION OF STATE POETRY SOCIETIES, INC.:
    Margit's Vienna, 1939
PACIFIC REVIEW: The Fishermen at Guasti Park
POETRY: A Door in the Wind, Return to Dresden, 1945
POETRY NORTHWEST: Master of the Wondrous Name
THE REAPER: Tat Tvam Asi, Epitaph
SHIRIM: Anonymous Lovers, Address to the Messiah,
    The Painting

The author wishes to thank friends and mentors whose remarks helped to sharpen the vision of these poems: Kimber Bentley, Robert Falk, Louise Glück, Garrett Hongo, Frances McConnel, Jim McMichael, Robert Mezey, Carol Muske, Barry and Grace Sanders, Cynthia Tuell, Dana White, and Charles Wright. And the author is most grateful to Bert Meyers, her silent mentor.

for

ROBERT, NAOMI, AND LEAH

Contents

Dream of the Red Chamber

Madras Bhavan

The Enchanted Room

Silhouettes

Dividing the Light

Dream of the Red Chamber

"As to the stories of breeze
and moonlight, they all deal
with such obvious things…"

—TSAO HSUEH-CHIN

A Door in the Wind

There was a time once when a door
in the wind opened up, and we
sailed through it effortlessly.
Nothing could stop us back then,
except the thought of stopping.

We open windows now, hoping the air
will whisper a clear summons
in our ears, but the wind seals
its lips, its stairways are forgotten.
Does it matter that we grow fond

of who we are, though we are different
than before? We forfeit old diversions
and open different doors. So devoted
to moving on, we move on; except now
and then, oh, the sighs in our hinges.

Master of the Wondrous Name

As a child he led the small ones
through the fields. Their voices
pierced the clouds flying toward heaven.
He spoke to the trees as a brother,
he saw the Enemy crouching behind light,
winding around the minds of men
like phylacteries, and enclosed
in the black heart of a werewolf.

Everything has a heart of its own,
said the Baal Shem Tov,
and every beast a wildly beautiful
song to release into the world.

Here a stone, a shoe, or a vase
filled with enviable flowers,
what do they say now?
That they have not been touched,
that they are filled with ennui,
that they await transformation
like all of us?

When he was dying, Rabbi Israel said,
The holy men after me will be
as leaves on trees, as numerous
as poppyseeds and as great.

Then in Poland, where life
in exile was like a dove
beating its wings against a storm,
the people danced and carried
their secrets folded up inside them
like pressed orchids in ancient books.

Still Life in Kitchen

She approaches the room as she would a lover.
Twilight follows her through aisles
over which solitude has slung its cover.
The floors are shoe-worn, etched with trials,
and above every age-crafted slat,
above the solid, dusk framed walls,
the moon hangs like a swollen bat.

On the stove, domes of ghostly pots
cast their shadows like hats against
the apricots and wan forget-me-nots.
Fragrances of dill and mint, condensed
into the vapors of hard blue light,
arouse the stillness of the room,
incite the clamorings of appetite.

This is the place of dreams,
a place of purpose, where sentiments
conspire with herbaceous schemes;
where the unfolding of events
suggests an ancient sybil's ritual;
where divinity rests in wine, salt, oil:
where sustenance becomes renewal.

There is something holy about food,
she muses, the way it passes through us.
Its purity assumes an attitude,
its impurity seems blasphemous.
She remembers the hen she plucked,
the disembowelment of a trout,
the bales of silken corn she shucked.

She stands now, above the steel sink,
bare feet planted firmly on cold tiles,
she looks out the window to an edge of pink
melting into earth, and she smiles.
Turning, she takes four plates in hand
and moves trancelike into the hushed yard,
and buries them in the still-warm sand.

Again and again she returns to replace
to earth the clay, now glazed and chipped
like yellowed teeth of a prehistoric race.
And if her thoughts have somehow slipped
away like swallows turning south:
tomorrow when she wakes at noon,
she'll find in every blade of grass
an open mouth.

Lost Souls in an Asylum

They are too recognizable this season,
appearing so much like us that we tip
our hats and cry out in one motion.

Some have found themselves held down
to their fates by only one thread:
loose buttons on a coat.

Others carry cups of water back
and forth, refusing to drink milk.
They all long for a father or mother.

They grow tired, now and then,
of being alone, of clenching both fists.
Let go, lost souls, of your pain.

They say: all we ever wanted from life
was a pair of good shoes and a song
that would heal us when we were down.

Slowly they move away, then stop to adjust
the sad expressions on their clothing.
Their eyes look through us.

They're everywhere out of their element,
they're floundering like fish:
they're voiceless and quietly ferocious.

Agent Orange

-- *for* D. R.

When Dick returned at last
and caught you up in his arms
to swing you over the tarmac,
you thought he hadn't changed a bit.
What a wedding it was: Uncle Felipe
bowlegged and toothless reliving
his ride with Pancho Villa,
the priest smoking Havana cigars,
and your mother lost in her own house,
her spiked heels in one hand,
an empty champagne bottle
wedged in her armpit.

But every night he saw it:
the explosion of flesh, and then
the fields charred and glowing.
For months Dick's screams
awakened you, and you bit
your nails into your palms
to keep from pushing him away.

When the baby was born dead
and faceless, you understood
something had gone wrong;
the rooms in the house sweated,
hot winds from the canyons
tore away every screen you put up.
You got pregnant again.

And this time no gifts from friends.
Your mother gone to China, trying
from the Great Wall to imagine Mao

on his pony looking back
over his shoulder at his rifle-
toting wife, and behind her
the thousands of peasants armed
with pitchforks and sticks.

On your mantle, the slender woman
in white smiles down innocently.
Ten years ago you hoped
you could make Dick whole again.
Now you eat and eat, your shadow
grown so large that he
can rock himself to sleep in it.

Uroboros

The wind's little brother visits the air.
His fragrance, hickory and cockspur.
I turn in my skin.
My belly plants its thumbprints,
my tongue splits.

I can taste the rocks working their way
blindly out of ground.
And though always hungry in the dark,
I wonder if what I put to my mouth
will be trapped in my jaws,
locked in my throat's clutch.

The wind's little sisters
stroke my back with their hair.
Pearly lights in my eyes shut off.
The moon's milk, a sweet venom,
fills my cup.

Dividing their music, the stars loosen
eels of light that undulate
through the parting grass.
My one light is a flame shuddering
in the pit of my tail.

My fangs carve themselves
toward my heart, and my hiss
is the last fire going out.

After I've swallowed my ashes,
I leave behind a halo of smoke.

Blue Movies

His fingers are caterpillars balanced
on the bough of her body.
Her legs snake around his trunk,
her arms entwine over his broad back.

The moans of the lovers float
above the heads of the Latino ushers,
past the ticket office where I.D. is required,
to the old men who are waiting in line
outside the theater in the black drizzle.
Some hold umbrellas as if they were candles,
others collect their breath in their hands.
One man studies a small red mole
protruding from the ticket taker's lip.

The line moves forward.
Thank you, they say, as they move out
of one darkness into another.

On the Island of Krk, 1971

In the olive trees
hundreds of cicadas
loosen their sprockets
as if to unwind the heat.

The sun burns another log,
littering cinders
over the green water.

Near my tent, swallows mate:
a scissor-shaped kite.

Everything is slow motion:
a boy and girl roll over
and over like wet laundry
in the cleansing surf.

Marbled pebbles swoosh and hiss
their little prophecies.

A single cloud tears itself
away from blue tarpaulins,

while slow tribes of red ants
carry off the Helens
of insect Troy.

Young men turning bronze
wonder what genies they'll unleash
when polished by love's hand.

Anonymous Lovers

Who are these who wait with bated breath,
rocking back and forth on their spines
like davening Hassidim at the Wall?

Some will call them nightmares
for the black muzzles they nudge in our ears,
for the hoofprints they leave in our sleep.

What a shame they can't speak to us
or give us their names, raised as if
for the blind, on embossed calling cards.

They are the ones we never wanted
to touch, the backward-looking glances
at love's absence, the freefall into earth.

Madras Insomnia

Struck head-on by the wind's blow,
two trees hum like tuning forks.
The sky's colander drains off
water from the stars while a parrot
sharpens its voice. A lone peacock
sputters in the dark.

I can't sleep under the fan's blades.
Saffron geckos cling upsidedown,
chirping and chirping for gnats.
Mosquitos unzip themselves from the wall.
Even the bee-eaters' slender tongues
untie their knots.

Outside, a banyan tree sinks its hooks
into an acre of dust. In the blue hills
langurs leaf through green crops,
and water buffalo sink into mud.
Spirals of light cling to night's ribs.
White ants spill out of bark.

I wish for the sleep of clear rivers,
for the midnight dreams of saints.
I wait to enter another realm where
one flame dances eternally on one toe:
where the bride of heaven sings a single note,
and the king cobra's hood cups the world.

Maṇalmēdu

The boy poses as a heron – all knees,
knuckles, talons – then scoops up a scorpion.

Saffron-clad, a solitary cloud meanders
along behind the sun's white mirage.

No noise from the rice paddies now,
no rains crashing through like elephants.

Banana trees flap their leaves to cool off,
a caterpillar ripples down an iron pump.

The boy tosses his scorpion upward
into an umbrella tree blackened by crows,

then strides down to the riverbed to sleep.
I sit tucked under the shade while days

of drought parade by on crooked feet:
holy men lost on their way to the sea.

Slowly, this waiting for rain piles up.
Andiappa, my landlord, dozes on a coir mat

next door, surrounded by plump grandsons,
roosters, and blue orchids.

Yesterday he told me that each man's fate
is a different colored stone plucked up

from the path that snakes through the forest
of illusions. He sleeps now, belly full.

The others, looming on the outskirts of hunger,
lash their arms together, and pray.

The Bearer's Son

Sundaram has stopped telling us
about the coconut lid on his hut,
how the rain rushes down
through palm fronds
in dirty waterfalls of light.

On a mat in the Harijan cērri
his son burned himself up with fever,
crying Ammā! and Rām!

Now, twelve hours later,
the funeral pyre pours its smoke
and sparks of bone
into the rose-watered air.
Bearing a gash of vermillion
and a blade of ash on his brow,
Sundaram weeps as he walks
along the rising river.

In Madras, monsoons repeat
themselves when no one is listening.
Droughts come and go
like missionaries bent
on conversion of the soil.
Children, named and loved,
their pockets empty, die of fever.

Eyes compressed, Sundaram returns:
his son's voice clenched in his teeth.

Next winter he will fire-walk
across a road tiled with red coals
as a penance to God.
And in his blood, year
after year, Sundaram
rehearses the dissolution
of the world.

HARIJAN CĒRRI: *untouchable village*
AMMĀ, RĀM: *Mother, God*

The Wedding

Her belly pushing open the door,
my sister carries her pride, wedges
it through the shuffling corridor
as petty bureaucrats peer over paper hedges
on dismal wooden desks, the hand-me-down
relics from the British Raj:
brass embossers, rubber stamps, pious frowns.

Khadi-clad, the groom trails behind
my mother with her Persian eyes;
my father flings the bitter rind
of an orange into a congregation of flies.
I bring two garlands heavy with jasmine,
and a ring the bearer resurrected
from a drawer at the last moment.

My sister's destination isn't this place
where endless forms are signed
and resignation repeats itself in every face.
She's looking for what she'll never find:
a man remade by formal acts,
unwavering as a signature,
a man unwedded to the past.

We encircle the snoring clerk.
My mother's sari sweeps his floor
and he awakens angrily, his chin jerks.
My office is my temple, he roars.
No one even snickers.
Our bodies barricade his shouts,
I see one garland begin to wither.

At last the clerk stammers out his task.
My sister's wedding over,
we kiss her over-flushed face and pat
the groom hastily on the shoulder.
He got what he wanted: a violin, a quest.
She, with her belly swelling in the heat,
has laid another part of herself to rest.

Yeti

In the blinding dawn,
villagers remove iron sickles
and shriveled scorpion plants
sewn to black sheets
in their doorways.

They cover the pits
of his enormous tracks
with their hands.

When they speak of him
their eyes narrow to a point.
Their hair, thickened with ghee,
stands straight on end.

During their sleep, girls wept,
dreaming their wombs
filled with his stench.

The shaman warns them to stay
in their huts, to avoid cats.
The girls whisper "dāg, dāg,"
fearing their souls
will be measured by threads,
then abducted.
They chant in hollow voices,
making themselves as small
as ghosts.

Tonight, when they fall asleep
at last, their souls will cling

to their bones: their terrified eyes
will clench, their skin
recoil from the touch
of his moon-white hair,
their hearts burst into flames.

Conversation in Madras

Twelve years ago my landlord,
Kalianasundaram,
told me his views about life.

I remember we munched on
polyunsaturated
cashews and sipped Bombay gin.

Mrs. Gandhi had proclaimed,
unconstitutionally,
a state of emergency.

She was a new Kālī, a
plenipotentiary
dictator, he said sadly.

What could I know of such things,
subequatorially
confined to this dialogue

that entwined the tales of gods,
anthropomorphically,
with the abuse of power?

Then I spoke of Nixon, so
unsophisticatedly.
And quite knowingly, he smiled.

Firewalking

A long strand of stars appears tonight
in the branches of the flame tree.

The moon, waking now from its eastern bed,
glides over the coals in a silver cloud of smoke.

The women go first with their palms raised
and their eyes glazed with love and their mouths

open slightly as if parted for a kiss. Then,
a flurry of adolescent girls, their saris

lifted above the knee, tucked into waistbands.
Some hold babies above their heads, and strangely,

the babies are quiet, even solemn, as they lift
their chins away from the incomprehensible heat.

Many are weeping now, weeping in joy,
in grief: old men who remember dancing above

the white ashes and who saw the goddess appear
with her necklace of skulls, with her six arms

beckoning them onward across past lives – and now
children whose tears trail amber lines on their skin.

Now the hush as the men tighten their dhotis
over their narrow hips and two from the temple

drag the goat squealing and baaing to the end
of the red glowing pit, and one throws up his arm

and the long blade falls swiftly through the neck
of the animal, and the animal's head rolls.

The old women take the head, take the body away.
And the sound begins to grow again, a chanting,

a frenzy of devotion, a swelling of joy; the sweat
covers their bodies in jeweled nets and their flesh

is so red their blood so red their voices rising
with the smoke, and their bodies, rapt with love,

form a string of dark pearls over the fiery coals,
and nothing pains them, nothing, nothing at all.

Tat Tvam Asi

Above us the awakening sky grows warm,
the moon's crescent horn blows itself dim:

a Tamil fisherman poles his frail *kaṭṭumarām*
across a flight of clouds.

With its slim neck and face open as a child's,
the Bay of Bengal lays its head down in Adyar

in this lagoon with its teak pavilions
and dwarfed cashurina pines flush on the banks.

Two egrets, their legs dangling like sticks of incense,
trail smoky lines in the clear black water.

Perhaps Yeats in a cream-colored shirt
would have paused here once with Annie Besant

to marvel at the flocks of birds spangling
the horizon with mango-red wings

or she, gripping the balsa rail, seeing the clouds'
turbans unravel in spools of silk, would have smiled.

There in the water's pasture our images
shift from foot to foot and fracture

while we hang motionless above the water's eye,
our bodies two shadows on a bridge.

This is the year I'd step out of myself
if I could, barefoot and without a passport,

arriving at this place, an infinitesimal ache
pressing its lips to my throat,

the sky's bowl of alms emptying itself into water,
the water's opus of light opening like a lotus.

TAT TVAM ASI: *that thou art*
KATTUMARĀM: *catamaran*

Sunrise on Kovalam Beach

The sea awakens you.
Beyond the fringes of thatched roofs,
stars slide down the horizon
into the sun's glare.

You rise, wrap a dhoti around your thighs.
An invisible bird trills, then stops
as you move sleepily
toward the open window.

You see the long white beach where
ten fishermen, heaving a boat
out of the rising surf, disappear
for a moment.

Like a small brown sail,
your back leans slightly forward
to the breeze, your arms
fall to your sides, your breath subsides.

Something has caught you midway
between waking and sleeping: a hum
that lingers on like the last
note of a twilight raga,

so that all the world seems suspended
in ice, fresh and intact.
Years later you'll try to recover
that instant,

you will try to remember everything
that's lost – blue mists, ochre roses,
burnished rocks, and nothing will remain
but light.

THE ENCHANTED
ROOM

"The great path has no gates,
Thousands of roads enter it.
When one passes through this gateless gate
He walks freely between heaven and earth."

—ZEN KOAN

Tooth Fairy

On her wedding night, my mother
flattened herself into a needle
which my father then threaded
by drawing himself through its eye,
disappearing into the darkness of her body.
Then my mother hurled herself up
into the sky and hooked her hair
on the moon's nail.

Thus I was born both
out of that tranquility to which she
marooned herself, and out of an essence
of loss, that one-armed bandit.

I'm a beautiful sight:
a diadem of stars nest in my hair,
and my breasts are immaculate.
My eyes search the world's windows
for tiny boxes, handkerchiefs,
or bottles stashed under countless pillows.

A certain tautness around the lips,
a tension in the fist
tell me which children wait
on the edge of sleep for my visit.
I burrow my hand under their heads
and deftly extract what I need.
Grateful, I bend and kiss their pursed lips.
After tossing the teeth in my sack,
I flex my wings and rise

through the curtains, like a moth
chased by the flame of greed.

It's no secret what I do with the teeth:
I implant them in the mouths
of prophets, so their words forever
remain small, pure, unfinished.

Heat Wave

The ringers in the tower of noon
have left their places
vibrating with silence.
Someone holds a mirror
to the sky's mouth
and no breath fogs its surface.

Green girls who must fall
soon into the earth,
listen with cocked ears:
oh leaves, revive!

The singers in the moon's mansion
have arisen en masse:
a choir bottled in ice,
a floating glass eye
surveys the land locked in salt.

A spider folds up
her black knitting needles,
a man dawdles with a book
of matches, waiting for next month
to arrive like a distant cousin.

Under the flat, forgetful roads,
a menagerie of blackened tongues:
small bells tolling like rain.

Snapshot

Two bears wrestle on the granite steps
under the yew trees. A gypsy with a green
cigarette holds one by a rope and opens
his mouth to blow smoke rings.

The minarets over Istanbul shimmer
like needles poking through the morning haze.
Mother has gone to the bazaar for a samovar,
father looks through his camera bag.

Near the cemetery an old horse's withers
tremble with flies, and mourners in veils
look both ways before crossing the street.
The sky over the Bosphorus is a skullcap.

How many years ago this was: I was twenty
and fair game for street urchins.
I wouldn't have been thinking of bears,
nor of a prophet's beard in St. Sophia.

I was fixed to the sound of a single note
wailing through the corridors of air:
a disembodied voice stitching the throng
together, calling them to the mosque.

I stood there and pressed the shutter then,
catching my breath in the click
of exposure: the plaintive song dissolving
like a ribbon of smoke in the glare.

The Painting

Place a man in the foreground,
and a woman with white hands,
and a child whose face is a small town.

Let them live a full life
in the narrow space of a frame.
Give them good shelter, raspberries,
a brass plate engraved with their names.

Battalions of clouds clip the light,
fringed with cypress needles,
the mock-blue sky hems the hillsides.

Change the scenery to summer:
hot gusts of dry air lift the pollens,
a black dog barks at a tailless lizard.

She's staring out to sea,
her head is cocked, she's listening.
She remembers a word: coriander.
She forgets it just as quickly.

The child gathers marbles,
hums a tune about a locomotive.

And before long
it's autumn again in the canvas.
The woman purrs by the hearth, her arm
draped around a cushion.
The man fidgets

the fire with a poker, his back
turned away from us.

Brush on a winter pond cracked
into a vague map by a child's skates.
Whispering, the father leans down
to the corner where two horses stall.
He's promised them sugar to haul
their empty wagon to the field.

Their day's finally over,
they darken and disappear.

The painted sky goes up in flames
as we move slowly
from room to room, dragging
our shadows along.

Zeitgeist

Distance yourself from the house
where the yellow roses bear a single fruit,

where the watchful dog howls at the moon
and children grow fat as new potatoes.

That is another life, a dark place
of mourning, a bitter wound in the side.

We have all been there at least once
before, or in our imaginings, and we know it

corner to corner as we know the contours
of our own faces and the hollows in our beds.

We've seen the stout warriors embossed
on copper plates and waistcoated shepherds

etched upon steins who make eyes
at the peasant girl frozen by Vermeer

in the act of pouring out her days;
we have tiptoed down cold cellar stairs

before sunrise to count our hidden gold,
to undress the barber's lame daughter.

That house is a wilderness to us, a miracle
we can't forget because we haunt it

with our arms outstretched blindly.
Those children with their rushed prayers,

those fathers with one hand tenderly cupped
on the nape of a small neck, and one fingernail

piercing an invisible calf, those sisters
roping their hair with the hangman's skill:

they are our family, bruises in the windows
who look out to witness our naked faces

as we stand on the outskirts of Eden,
blackening the walls with our cries.

The Origin of Death

Once upon a time someone died. And because it was the first death, the universe was stunned; the trees in woods threw off their needle cloaks in dark despair, the many creatures, near and far, went into hiding behind clouds or under dry riverbeds: the people, still a bit stiff in clay suits, remolded their faces to register fear. A woman had stretched herself out like a long canoe on the shore, had merely closed her eyes and closed her lungs to breath.

A child approached the cold body of the woman. "Mother," she said. "Wake up. It's time to bring in the flock." Someone in a bush nearby cleared his throat. Someone else felt, for the first time, the trickle of warm water leak from his eyes. An armadillo sniffed the woman, then laid down its head at her feet. "Mother," the child said again. And when, for the third time the child addressed the woman and heard no answer, she walked away, down to the tidepools to gather shells.

This all happened so long ago that even fossils, with their hardy, imprinted stories, argue over the details. But it has been said things changed after that. Nervousness and impatience were born. Swallows migrated south in winter. Sharks grew teeth. Bananas grew dark spots. And young armadillos thickened their hides. No one lived happily ever after, except the child, whose heart beats on, and who sees her mother in every stone.

The Sibyl

When I was a small girl of modest words, I thought
the fluted music rising up from under the hedgerows

to be no more than water traveling the roots, singing
over rocks as it moved silkily underground.

And those voices in the night, well, I believed
black swans had gathered in the garden font,

or thought perhaps the stars were chattering again
like a dawn procession of wives gone for the day's fish

to that market propped up at the horizon's gate.
Such sounds were the riddles of my youth, vague cures

for boredom while my brothers sailed their reed boats.
Now my days are littered with worries, despite the gold

light upon my arms, the masked adulation of priests.
For I know even Apollo's flattery couldn't save

Deiphobe from being strung up, finally, from a nail,
a captive in a bottle, condemned to wither into air.

Beloved of goats, what kind of lie is this I live?
Each prophecy I make is only a thimble of wisdom,

a sip of honey, one quick blink of clarity,
among a bewilderment of portents, omens, sighs.

Soon they will tire of me and cast me off like cat-gut
from a broken string. Nothing else sustains me now

but the rhythm of their prayers, the burning rain, darts
of their cold tongues upon my thighs, their fingertips

rousing my breasts, the forked melody of an aulos
splitting each night open, my body inflamed, my throat

thrown back as some god explodes from my lips, while
my own voice hides in the folds of my other mouth.

Mittleschmerz

Halfway through the narrow waist
of the hourglass, the sand thins
to a pause – time momentarily stops.
The moon points its divining rod at my thighs,
one ovary releases its dewdrop into the dark.

Halfway through the month, halfway through the year
that marks the middle of my league-long life,
I round myself out, I swell like a ball
of cotton dropped into water.
And my body becomes a bridge, a highway;
all my rivers are singing, singing.

Only now, when my womb awaits its pearl,
when I'm ablush with desire, only now
do I feel the tremors of the dead.
Their sterile harvest stiffens my joints;
their noisy silence pulls my breath back in.

Mother country, where is the map?
I still don't know what my body knows,
nor can I postpone my bewilderment.
The flesh and blood of my life snap back:
but my spirit, whatever a spirit is,
waits for one more chance to break out.

MITTLESCHMERZ: *"middle sorrow," ovulation*

The Fishermen at Guasti Park

In the first days of summer
the three elms, those slightly
opened fans, unfold
their shadows across the river.
Two dogs arrive exhausted,
tongues dripping, and settle
down near the frogbait jars.
Aiming their poles
toward the center of water,
the Sunday fishermen watch
the light pirouette off
the opposite shore.
Their wives peel onions,
open wine, do their nails.
Most of the men think
as little about gravity
as they do about war and
the weightlessness of time.
How could they know that
it is only the single, collective
thought of their abandoned childhoods
that keeps the world afloat?

The Enchanted Room

The deer is not only a deer but a woman.
Its hooves tattoo the pink walls.

The lion is not only a lion but a man.
Its mane rises like the sun.

They dance on hind legs under a chandelier.
The ceiling is singed, the walls dimple.

Her eyes are veiled by a skin.
His teeth surrender to a slow smile.

Soon they'll breed many children.
Owls, snakes, and minks slip from her loins.

He roars now and then for effect.
The children nibble at the corners.

She thinks the room is too small, a trap.
He plays tic-tac-toe in his den.

The room glows like a mad hornet:
it doesn't let anyone else in.

SILHOUETTES

"Je rêvais croisades, voyages de
découvertes dont on n'a pas de
relations, républiques sans histoires,
guerres de religion étouffées,
révolutions de mœrs, déplacements
de races et de continents: je croyais
à tous les enchantements."

"I dreamt of crusades, voyages of
discoveries of which there are no
reports, republics without recorded
histories, suppressed religious wars,
moral revolutions, movements of races
and of continents: I believed
in all enchantments."

—ARTHUR RIMBAUD

Conversation with Wang Wei

Fish play east of the lotus,
Fish play west of the lotus.

I have hitched the cart
near the grove of Five Willows
but you, friend, sit idly by
with your thin ankles
ringed by green water.

You spread a handkerchief
over the ripples
so that dragonflies can rest
their wings as you paint them.

Have you heard yet
about those men who strolled
across the moon's surface?
For days lake tides reeled
and women hung by open windows
staring past cobwebs
of starlight
enshrouding the passion vines.

Nothing changes, you say,
but the nature of yearning.

Your painted scrolls,
alive with floating clouds,
dip their prows
in the Wang River
and are forgotten.
Fancying themselves poets,

fishermen sing drunkenly
about hauling the moon in
at low tide.

Soon monks in poppy-colored robes
pound the dinner gongs.
My little horse paws
the duckweed.

As you put away your brushes
you say, never mind
the moon, the lost riches.

And your voice, like a tuft
of milkweed shaken loose
by the wind's fingers,
fades into the blue air.

Margit's Vienna, 1939

On these naked October nights
when shivering trees release their leaves,
I watch the moonlight shift
and fall into a frozen sleep,
while dull winds cut across the west.
Ice surrounds the distant stars
and halos them with light and death.

Here in my flanneled fright,
I see the curtained town in disbelief.
Iron wings fold in upon the nest;
birds of prey, neighbors count our teeth.
They want our gold, my satin dress,
they'll smile and joke about the war,
and curse this house beneath their breath.

Each face darkens the glass: a blight
spreads that no one sees or heeds;
neighbor and friend, even our cypress
bends itself into a poisoned weed.
I feel the ache of October in my breast,
and the sweet years glower
irretrievably, like the dead.

Don't tell me that all autumn nights
have shuttered eyes, that every tree
casts off its homeless leaves; what's best
is lost...but oh, October, remember us, how we
gazed at empty trains weighted down with frost:
remember our lights lit the corridors
of gloom, as we vanished like silhouettes.

Volga Tale, 1944

They have trudged for hours across the glassy river;
the child silent, the woman and man silent.
Around them the trees circling the shore
are a barbed necklace of towers,
and the sky dingy as dishwater.
Though it's been carved down to a rib,
the moon follows them like a steady friend.
Once, when the child looks down, he sees
a dead wolf frozen beneath the floor of ice,
its corpse huge and blue under the lantern.

At dawn they divide their last turnip,
and cut their conversation thinly into slices.
Petty tyrants, the birds hover on the edge
of their sputtering campfire, eyeing their mouths.
The woman's skinny fingers pluck like needles
at the boy's scalp; she flicks the lice to the birds.
Inside the boy's pocket is a pencil box.
Inside that is the wishbone of a chicken
whose good luck has kept them alive for months.
Often he's dreamed of eating it.

The cold is a winding sheet fitted to their skins.
Why will God have them suffer? the boy wonders
as they move across the river's clouded mirror.
Suddenly, he sees before him a holy figure
floating, glowing like an ember.
The white robes billow like curtains as
the boy stumbles forward, smiling.
But the figure has taken out his pistol, and
by the time the report of the explosion reaches
the boy's ears, the boy is kneeling.

Oh mother, oh father, cries the boy
as the soldier hugs him to his frost-covered coat.
I was mad, mad with hunger, the stranger says.
Please forgive me, the stranger begs.
The boy looks at him in joy, his beautiful face
lost in joy, his beautiful eyes closing their windows.
On the river's other side there'll be fresh milk
for him, and a basket filled with violets.
But for now, there's only the silence of the birds,
and the sound of a wolf baying under the ice.

A Moment in Time,
while Cynthia Awaits Labor

It's always the same story, you yearn
for a transparent dream, for an unwinding

passion that lives on the inside of the skin,
for a prayer that changes from water

into blood, from nerves into quicksilver.
You crave a hymn for your drowning.

Now you must learn another way to walk,
a new way of pulling things out of yourself,

you must learn to sing lullabies in the night,
and remind yourself of the power of your left hand,

of the curious clothes a woman tears off
when her body grips her.

The Soldier

They say my hands are machines,
oiled with blood.
They press me to guard the horizons,
to wash my hands with mud.
Taught not to question a cause,
just to die, my life becomes
a series of simple acts.

Keep your head empty, they say,
and your hair cut close to your scalp:
hide your birth marks so that the enemy
won't recognize you as himself.

I change the rules to fit my silence.
I carry the hope for a long life ,
at the bottom of my sagging heart.
My fingers aren't bullets, but vines;
and when I lean on my rifle at sunset
I feel like a farmer.

No one knows how I pay for doubt.
I try to measure everything I've done,
but in 18 years everything I've earned
is lint in my pockets.

Still, here I am, and how can I
confess my sins to come, knowing
that they will last forever?
What comes from my actions

is for the good of the world, they say.
And I try to love my destiny.

But I would rather be deceived, admit
I like my boots, and the rhythm of a march,
even the food, and the endless jokes
about the colonel's tiny prick.

They tell me, oil your machines,
keep them clean.
But the truth of the matter is:
their eyes don't cry,
their hearts have dried up
like severed figs,
and to ask them for reasons
would be like asking a dying man
what time it is.

The Skeletons in the Closet

They sit politely behind the dresses,
fumbling through pockets, fingering
the seams of evening gowns, looking
not for a way in, but for a way out.

How smooth their bones, like alabaster
shaved from moonlight; the digits
of their toes look like broken bits
of blade from a Lilliputian's sword.

What a handsome family they are:
it's as if all their imperfections
had fallen away with their flesh,
it's as if they're finally perfect.

But how they beg me to let them out.
They say my closet is a flophouse,
they threaten to put on wedding clothes
or crash down the door when I'm naked.

But I resist such threats and ploys;
I'm no fool, and I know them well.
When they whisper in falsetto voices
it's to declare another war, or else,

brittle and bowlegged, they'll dance
in between the slacks and overcoats;
they'll sing lewd songs and chew up
my leather gloves, my ostrich boa.

At night they scratch their long nails
across the floor like white chalk

upon a blackboard, and they hiss and
sputter like hot oil dropped in water.

When they think I'm asleep, I tiptoe
to the keyhole to watch them feed
on tear-stained sleeves and dirty laundry.
Such things give them back their power.

Return to Dresden, 1945

– for the Idelovici family,
    killed in the firebombing of Dresden

The road is a ribbon of moonlight
threading darkness to darkness.
Shadows peel themselves out from trees;
we waver, then pass through them.

We're going home.
No one thought we'd make it
past the Czech border, being shoeless,
unarmed, our passports long ago bartered.

Behind us, pyramids of munitions gleam
from huge pallets: six years,
a wealth of lives stacked in weapons.
We leave Theresienstadt to the wolves.

Yesterday we left two children in the woods.
Now we try to muffle their hearts
which throb in our ears, which blind us.
We buried ourselves in the woods.

Just place one foot
in front of the other, brother.
Your simplest act of breathing
suffocates these angry shadows.

We know we'll be unrecognizable
with our closed faces, our hoarse voices.

We were always unwelcome, but perhaps
tonight we'll inherit the earth.

We've learned that everything is possible,
that every road is an endless danger.
Up ahead the city glitters like heaven:
the Americans will save us.

Mystery of the Missing Wives

Husbands, every night we disappear.
Can you blame us?
Too much cold weather,
too few indigenous pleasures,
not enough power.

We disappear into laughter:
in the hallways we combust
like gunpowder.

Where have they gone this time,
you ask the children.

We confess: some nights
we take off our wifely clothes
and slip slowly into air.
Like watermarks in books,
we grow more subtle as we fade.

But it's a dangerous game we play;
our senses get blurred,
and worse: when we return to you
we see only the world's smallness,
its bald spots and arrogance,
the splinters in the cross.

Sometimes we don't come back
all of one mind.

Sometimes we find that
while we're gone our children

fall into decline.

Fishscales of light trickle
from their eyes,
and they mouth little o's
of despair as they swim circles
beneath us in the dark.

Loved ones, do not doubt us;
for though our love is indecipherable
as death, it is more permanent.
We love you all whether
we are there or not.

Believe us when we say we die
in thimblesful for you, or
that we love you blindfolded,
with our hands
tied behind our backs.

It's just that we yearn
for unencumbered selves,
and walk through walls to find them.

So, farewell again.
We leave a trail of skins
behind us.

Numerical Bestiary

1 was a wise old man with a fang.
2 was a swan who never flew.
3 mothered fraternal twins.
4 lost an arm in the war.
5 talked too much, became a star.
6 stood on his head to meditate.
7 was full of magic and sins.
8 learned how to figure skate.
9 had a swell head.
10 was the one who married none.

Night

Dusk blues the trees,
the solemn moon lights
candelabras in the reeds:
everything's part of night.

Fireflies freed from a jar:
the stars zigzag wildly
and flicker their icy hearts.
Behind the horizon a jaguar

crouches ready to fling
its paws over great waters.
Hold still, dark wings
grasp the grasshopper

to make it trill and trill.
Black winds rotate the sky,
transform the marbled hills
until they are part of night.

And near the house's eaves
the grinding day begins
to lift the carob's leaves
like paper cherubim

into its toiling arms.
Speak black tongues: unite,
until each daybreak swarms
like another part of night.

Dividing
the Light

"Love is in the house
of the body of the poem.
When one passes through this gateless gate
He walks freely between heaven and earth."

—JACK HIRSCHMAN

The Burning Rose

At midnight a burning rose appears
in the mouth of the blackened fireplace.

The father stares into its center
and sees himself dying
under the spokes of the sun's wheel.

Still wearing the pearls her grandmother
once pressed into her hands,
the mother watches the petals of fire
whiten with age, curl into thorns.

The child, running her fingers up
and down the coarse spine of the dog,
thinks she sees a brilliant umbrella opening,
an umbrella with all the sunsets
in it, and she laughs.

But her laughter stays close
to her lips, and unlike smoke,
refuses to rise above her head.

Dividing the Light

Mother, antique clouds prowl the heavens
and the moon is balanced on the far side
of the house, waiting for some sign
before it puts up its white flag.

Moisture clamps itself to the window.
A row of potted violets waits patiently
for my hands to hover over them.
It is quiet both inside and out tonight.

But let me describe the scene again:
behind me, in the small room
of childhood, I hear father playing
Liszt on the piano while you stare
vacantly, as I do now,
out through a telescope of windows.

This is what you taught me:
that life is a blue rag to shake out,
put away, admire.
Our time here is too short.

Another winter closes its shutters,
and spring nuzzles against my hair.
All the newspapers are glazed with sorrow:
let them burn away with winter
in the open fireplace.

Mother, you once told me that
the world was too much with me.
But how can I shake it off now,
being thirty-two and still at loose ends?

We whittle our lives away to the bone,
dividing the light
into separate rooms of memory.
Was I your child once,
or you mine?
Let's sit and watch winter turn
the corner on its way south,
let's stop measuring out
the portions of change.

See how the wind shuttles across
the apricot's branches, tearing down
handsful of snowy blossoms?
The black field of grass
is littered with white lions.

Confession

Tell me, father, why did you leave me
every night, your finger cocked
on your keyring, your blue eyes drifting
toward the door as you waltzed out?
You left me long before the pink letters
came floating down the mail slot, long
before the year mother lost her mind
and dressed up in petticoats and ribbons
only to sit by a window and sink
into the whirlpool of depression.
You abandoned me at birth, seeing that I
was an absence, another girl.

I find forgiveness hard to bear.
It should start somewhere near the heart
and spread its anesthesia into the lungs,
then through the bowels, and upward
to the mind, where it numbs even
the tiniest synapse between words.
But my urge is something only my fingers
can tap out, blindly, obediently,
without linking thought to touch.
You left me daily to my own sorrow;
for if you loved me, you did so silently,
behind the closed door of your solitude.

Even the pride you'd wanted to squander
on a son has rounded edges now,
and seems so worthless. Am I, to you,
a stranger from the past who blocks
every exit, who blows the smoke of remembrance
in your face? I was your burden, you

my hope; but now I see your life trailing
behind you, the faint tail of a comet
long extinguished. I feel your pain: that clot
that grows as it travels the body's house.
We're nothing if not children of our losses:
you, crying too often; me, not crying enough.

Wintering In

Donna Lucia taught me how to knit
in Fontaine la Port when I was seven.

We lived in Maurice Chevalier's summer house,
which clung to the wooded hill like a nest.

My French was poor, as was hers, and so
we conversed discreetly in Italian during

the winter months of mud and influenza,
when my parents buttoned themselves into books.

In love, she said, with a man who owned a red car,
his name bothered by many rolled R's, Lucia

sang her contagious song into my ear
all December while I knitted a misshapen snake.

I wore it later coiled around my neck on jaunts
down to the apple orchards by the Seine.

My sister was busy with dreams of Jeanne d'Arc,
and with two foul-mouthed boys who taught her

how to say fornicate in French, and how to kiss
using her tongue as a soft dart.

Donna Lucia cooked with too much garlic:
my skin grew white, or so I thought.

We both loved to eat it raw, and so everyone
avoided our secrets, except the dog.

But best of all, Lucia taught me how to count
lost stitches of yarn, and how Italian

sweetens the tongue like the taste
of pungent, grey afternoons when we waited

to catch sight of a red Fiat, as it threaded
its way over the neck of the horizon.

Being Eight

She is furious.
Caught by the iron claw of the bed,
she sits on the floor beside a pudgy doll
to rock back and forth over the injured knee.
Why don't you ever listen to me? she yells,
and the row of sad-eyed tigers and bears
nod their bowed heads, as her hot tears fall.
Being eight isn't easy.
I remember the quiet anger of failure,
the loud anger, the shy fear of danger,
the errors of my body: headaches, stomach aches,
still too much baby fat everywhere.

I want a fence around my room,
around my bed, she says, and already
she's pulling off her blue socks,
wrapping them around the sharp metal corner
that stabbed her, mid-run, as she tried
to escape my poorly timed humor, my hug.
But the fury still simmers and quite suddenly
I remember her birthday – the drive on the freeway
to the rink, and next to us the rig
with its fenced-in cargo;
the bug-eyed calves pressed flank to flank,
their mouths open, their nostrils flared.
Mommy, where are they going? she asked
over the roar of terrified mooing and traffic.
And when I told her
she cried with such astonishment,
such fury that no one remembers
the gifts, the party guests,
the ride home.

November Ellipsis

The autumn that the *Dominator* lost its way
in the fog and smashed its iron hull
against the crumbling peninsula,
and all night long we heard
the slow moan from the lighthouse horn,
that autumn held almost too much joy for us.
It was the year everything went wrong
except the light that reared
off the black waves and rode in armies
down the sand-swept boulevards,
that saddled the sleeping bums in brocade
and hammered the stars dangerously
close to the horizon.
From our rooftop crow's nest, where Job's
plaster shadow fell between the slats,
we watched the light unhinge the leaves
one by one and reshingle each barren branch.
My sister's moonwhite legs dangled
like bait from the low-rimmed deck
as currents of blue mist billowed in.
Poised in her flannel gown over the edge
of a vacant world, she unraveled
the mysteries of sex to me: how the body
combusts from the first kiss, how a boy's hands
drowsily initiate the flesh, how sublime,
how cruel that entry into ourselves is.
Peering at me through the spellbound light,
her face became clearer, and something
flowered in the autumn fog,

a kind of softening of disaster.
Far off the lip of King Harbor,
the ship that ran aground loosened
its cargo and drowned itself gracefully
in the sea's contours.

Red Tide

During August, when the ocean thickens
with plankton, when saltgrass
and pickleweed lie low,
my sister and I drift out
of the house in our nightgowns.

We leave no trace on the strand
as we weave our bicycles
along the shrouded shorefront
that leads to King Harbor.

Every night seems a full moon night
as we balance our weight in the sabot,
then slip through the black corrals of water.

Stars pinned to the moist sky
beat their wings furiously,
while the man in the moon tilts
the mast, his features scumbled by fog.

Waves light up like neon wires,
then blink on and off the shoreline.
Our boat drifts in circles,
its rigging slack.

On shore, silver flames erupt
and taper out of the surf
to flicker there like myriad tongues;

but it's only the grunion
running aground again.

I watch our wake erase itself,
the flimsy prow dipping and rising
out of light-spattered shallows,
my sister slowly pawing the water.

Hermosa Beach, Revisited

Seastorms throttle the far breakwater,
and here by the light-flayed pier,
small, greedy waves continue
to burst out of brief composure.

This slow journey I make against
the hunched wind is one of recovery.
What did I know? What didn't I know?
I follow the sea's refrain lazily.

Sandpipers, transient terns, gulls
crowd, cross, pass, and stroll,
ruffling the sand, retelling history
before the stroke of the seventh wave.

Some things never seem to change.
Dewey still scowls above the strand
behind clear glass: his proud belly,
a can of Coors clasped in his hand.

There's Karate Joe's driftwood bungalow
wedged like a barnacle between pilings
of two houses near the wide esplanade.
And Mrs. Cronmiller in a nightgown

brushing down her knee-length white hair,
then wrapping it in a newspaper hat.
She's gone, and now the ocean mimics
her, combing out snarls of white froth.

These faces are immaculate now
in my mind, each memory a delicate shell
whose tenant has moved on. Still,
I'm here, where I first learned to love

this forlorn mazarine sky, so wise
in its unnerving calm, the fallen clouds
breaking apart on shore, and the sea
owning it all, reclaiming everything:

the slow merger of dark into dark,
small furnishings of silence forever
inhabiting the past, and the crying out
of great gulls fading into it.

Venice, 1959

I want to be the woman who leans
languidly in the doorway of the church,
her black hair loose about her face,
her spiked heels red as lobsters.

But I am only nine, and wear cotton
sundresses my mother bought for a song
in Rome last winter. A grey cloud
of pigeons stares at my hands,

while a few alight on my shoulders,
mistaking me for a tiny madonna.
The canals are bright lines of water
broken up by the bobbing cries of sailors

shortchanged by weather or by lovers.
Beyond my small bones of the moment
lies the world of illusions: the sun's hands
scattering its coins in a fountain's bowl

as soapstone dolphins leap in place,
trying to flee the gargoyles' lewd display
of teeth. And I, my arms burnt sienna,
my sighs ruffling the birds' feathers,

watch the full lips of sunlight press against
a golden cross, as a clear carafe of wind
empties itself. And the beautiful woman,
her round hips swaying, enters the dark.

We Are Still

unwinding the war, as if it were
a great spool of copper wire
squeezed out of the grave's cornucopia:
one inch, one year, one link
and Mike McCann rolls out, big-handed,
buck-toothed, his year-old mustache
stiffening, his purple heart clanging
like a dinner bell.

I should have married him,
or at least climbed him
to the pier's altar to say
I'd push him over the ledge
if he went off to fight.
Instead, I stepped down
the salty stairs to guilt,
while he went off
like a bullet.

Oh, I repent.
I am a hostage to my bed,
while he withdraws his hands
into the stillborn elements,
his voice embalmed, his chin,
knuckles, toes rubbed smooth
as a rigid umbilicus.

Each hour his name's read aloud
from a list of the day's casualties;
he's another mint-fresh dollar
coughed out of the furnace.

We can't turn anger back to flesh.
We've spent our breath
on useless incantations.
We are not alchemists.
The groom is dead, the bride
recoils from innocence.

The war left us in pieces:
that hasty marriage with its dowry
of orphaned children, flames,
and empty promises,
with its too-tight wedding band
cutting off our blood.

Winter Song

Hope is an ornament of stone,
the graveyard's diadem.
It grips my daughter's palms
to its pure white heart.

She, who survived the long hard
stare of death, and even smiled
back into its eyes,
not recognizing that icy face:
she knows, and so do I.

We need the blindfolded dove
of hope unleashed
from the weathered trunk of despair,
drawn out like a breath
from the dilemma of flesh;

the distillation of fire,
the hieroglyphics of soil
rewired into tendrils, blossoms:

in hope the music of no-man's-land
becomes a canonized song,
the slow hours of tunneling
through mazes of iron walls
give burst to sudden insight,

as when the sun returns each day
to make its morning repairs,
to secure bright icons
in the blue iris of the air.

Seizure

This falling away from the world
is a death you perform
like a marionette dangled in a room
who slips from the strings and crossbar
of love, and crumples into wooden imposture.
I would float you back into your skin
if I could, and pump my breath
into your lungs until they steadied us both.
But already as I reach, you pull
apart from my voice, you fade on the bed.

Come back,
return to your child's body
and this four-cornered light,
to my hand paused
over your brow like a rag.

Where do I go to retrieve you?
Your absence blackens the windows.

This falling away from my world
wrenches you into someone else.
I want to shake the cruel grin
off your face and break your arms
from their flight.

I am wingless, grounded.
I will have you as you are,
Naomi, and I'll press your stiff body
like a splinter into mine.

Women at Thirty

Women at thirty
Learn to swing slightly
In the hinges of their steps
As they ascend.

At ease on the carpeting
They feel it gliding
Beneath them now like an air-borne sail,
Though its speed is slowed down.

And deep in mirrors
They recover
The face of the girl as she tries on
Her mother's smile and kisses

The face of that mother
Still warmed by the mystery of father.
They are more and more women now.
Something is touching them, something

That is like the sun's brush
Of white light, minute,
Unfurling the ferns at the base of the yard
Beyond their children's windows.

(After a poem by Donald Justice.)

Address to the Messiah

I have shrugged off the absence
of God, that black chasm handed down
like a boot from my father,
used to kick away traditions.
I've inherited from my mother
a curious need for sabbath candles,
though they go unlit.

Who are you, with wings spread thin
as a poor man's butter?
I watch you roll the full moon
across the sky, when stars blank out
like errors, entering wisdom in lost books.
I dream of flying past galaxies
of faceless women: you hold me by a string
and swing me over the horizon,
my feet dangling like hooks.

In ashen fields I drag these feet
like a curse over a patchwork of graves.
I find you cowering
under some golden nettles.
What a shoddy thing you are: soiled,
culled from raked bones,
a worm-eaten cabbage.

Now I dress myself in white lies,
in the necklace of your fingerprints.
Fumbling, I put on your shroud,

your wedding gown.
I know you are the backward glance,
the dead weight of passion, the face
gone white that glows behind the mirror:

and I am the candle
that lights itself with dark.

Garden Twilight

The seeds that rot
underground are not lost
but are merely absorbed,
like hosts.

They are certain
syllables that join
themselves humbly
to others,
doing the work
that never comes
to fruition,
of itself.

They go unnoticed,
these seeds,
or else worms take them
in and push them out
again, or the wind
lifts their cover
and carries them
across town.

What seeds sprout
take strength
from the others' absence,
the way we lean now
on our spades,
looking west

to where the sun
has fallen.

It's as if we
had forgotten something,
and so bend our ears
not to the ground,
but to the distance
past the horizon.

That's the only place
where absence
has both a shape
and a small sound:

where the sun
balances itself
on the tip
of our lives,
before darkness
works us back
into darkness.

Epitaph

Remember the black confetti
of sparrows released into clouds,

and the swivel-headed mantis
rotating its eyes like a madman;

remember the uprooted sapling
leaving its invisible claw in earth,

the double helix of lives
that vanishes with the scythe;

remember a thousand little bells
singing like river angels,

the heaving galaxies lifting
sequins of water from girls' eyes,

and the pollen of plundered bone
shifting its footprints underground.

PAGE 10

The Baal Shem Tov was an 18th century Jewish mystic who is credited with renewing the spirit of Judaism in Eastern Europe.

PAGE 17

An uroboros is the circular symbol of a snake swallowing its own tail.

PAGE 19

Krk is an island located just off the coast of Yugoslavia.

PAGE 26

Manalmēdu, a small village in South India, means "sand pile" in Tamil. Coir is a woven material extracted from coconut husks.

PAGE 28

In an Indian household a bearer serves the same function as a butler.

PAGE 30

Khadi is the handspun cloth worn by Gandhi and millions of Indians.

PAGE 32

A yeti is known in the west as Sasquatch, Big Foot, and the Abominable Snowman. "Dāg" is witchcraft.

PAGE 37

Tat tvam asi (Sanskrit) is a phrase drawn from the ancient Chandobya Upanishad. Each section of this chapter closes with a father instructing his son: "Sarvam tat satyam sa ātmā *tat tvam asi* Śvetaketu iti." ("All is that truth. He is the soul, *that thou art*, oh Śvetaketu.") I am indebted to Robert Falk for his translation.

PAGE 39

A dhoti is a length of cloth, usually khadi, which South Indian men wear wrapped around the lower half of their bodies.

PAGE 53

An aulos is an ancient double-reed flute, which was the principle wind instrument used by the Greeks.

PAGE 59

Wang Wei (A.D. 699-761) was a Chinese poet and a devout Buddhist.

PAGE 61

For Margit and Martin Falk.

PAGE 64

For Cynthia Tuell.

PAGE 73

Each Arabic numeral which opens a line is followed by a description of the number's shape. Line 7 is an exception.

PAGE 85

The *Dominator*, a large cargo ship, met its demise off the tip of Palos Verdes, California, in 1963. It was carrying tapioca, which grew too damp, swelled, and cracked the hull.

PAGE 92

For Michael McCann (1949-1968).

Maurya Simon was born in New York City in 1950 and grew up in Europe and Southern California. She was educated at the University of California, Berkeley, and at Pitzer College, and holds an M.F.A. from the University of California at Irvine. In the early 1970s, she lived in India where she studied Tamil. In 1983, she won a University Award from the Academy of American Poets. She presently teaches at Scripps College and lives with her husband and two daughters on Mount Baldy, California.